# LIVING BEYOND SIGHT

It Don't Take Eyes For Everything

**TYRON TROTTER**

Copyright © 2024
TYRON TROTTER
Living Beyond Sight
*It Don't Take Eyes For Everything*
All rights reserved.

No part of this publication may be reproduced, distributed, or transmitted in any form or by any means, including photocopying, recording, or other electronic or mechanical methods, without the prior written permission of the author, except in the case of brief quotations embodied in critical reviews and certain other non-commercial uses permitted by copyright law.

TYRON TROTTER

Printed Worldwide
First Printing 2024
First Edition 2024

10 9 8 7 6 5 4 3 2 1

# LIVING BEYOND SIGHT

# Table of Contents

About the Author .......................................................................... 1

Introduction ................................................................................ 3

Chapter I: From the Plantation to the Hill ............................... 5

Chapter II: School for the Blind ............................................... 37

Chapter III: Southern University ............................................. 57

Chapter IV: Historical Pioneer ................................................. 81

# About the Author

Ty is a member of the National Federation of the Blind and was also a member of the American Council for the Blind, along with his mother Sandra. His mom is the only blind NFB member in his family. However, with his extended blind family, Ty has learned people are people. Love, respect, and opportunity are things that everybody wants, including the blind and visually impaired.

# Introduction

In 2020, I had the opportunity to get to know a historical pioneer of the East Baton Rouge Parish school system. This trailblazer was the first totally blind schoolteacher in East Baton Rouge Parish. She worked in that school system for 15 years. I have known her most, if not all, my life. This teacher helped me become the person I am now.

You see, that teacher is my mom. Since she raised me, I assumed that I knew everything about her. However, my opinion changed one Saturday morning while we were sitting at her dining room table enjoying a cup of coffee. At that time, I was writing and publishing a book called *Barber Life: The Shop Hopper*. That morning, we talked about many things.

One of those topics was her life before I was born. Before long, our morning coffee talks became a routine, and they no longer happened only on Saturdays. During this time, I developed a renewed admiration for my mom (along with a new coffee habit) as she told me about the challenges she overcame.

Looking back, I think my mom was finally ready to have her story told back then. She has said many times she would like to write a book, but she was just too lazy to.

After months of being reintroduced to my mom, I began to record our coffee talks and now I am sharing them with you, the reader and listener of this book, in her own words. Thank you, all.

# Chapter I

## From the Plantation to the Hill

I was born in Coushatta, LA. It is a small town in the northwestern corner of the state. It is about 50 miles south of Shreveport and just about 20 miles north of Natchitoches. I was a foster child; however, I did not know this until I was a grown woman. I always refer to myself as being raised by Emma and James "Jimmy" King.

I was born to a 20-year-old lady named Carrie Lee Cole on May 12, 1950. It was on this day that I was accidentally dropped in a chamber pot, also known as a slop jar. Many people speculated that event was the cause of my blindness.

I never knew my real father. I stayed with Carrie Lee for six months.

Then, in January 1951, Emma and James King took me into their care. I called Emma King "Mama;" she was the only mama I ever knew. Mama Emma would go over to the house where Carrie Lee lived with my grandmother, Lucy Bell, to visit an elderly aunt of

Jimmy's. Mama was no blood kin of mine, but Daddy was first cousins with my great-grandfather, Jessie Lawson.

When she saw me, Mama thought I was small for a 7-month-old. Frequently, she would see me in a rocker with wet clothes.

Around that time, Mama noticed my eyes did not focus right. She asked Carrie Lee's family about it. They did not know because they never took me to a doctor.

In passing, people would say jokingly, "Give me that baby!"

However, when Mama said those words, Carrie Lee took the offer seriously. It was almost Christmas, and Mama did not expect to hear a yes.

Mama replied, "I have to wait until after Christmas."

She really had to get Jimmy's head right. She needed to convince Jimmy to take in another child. Jimmy was already upset with Mama Emma for taking in his great-nephews. He wanted to know why Emma was going around picking up other people's responsibilities.

## I. FROM THE PLANTATION TO THE HILL

I was very sickly, unable to eat anything. Mama turned to her faith in God. Mama believed her faith is what saved me. One night, I looked so lethargic and very sick, but the next morning I was cooing and playing. She also believed God had made me come to her, so she could raise me to be a good person.

Once Emma and Jimmy decided to raise me, a friend of the family asked Mama, "Emma, what are you going to do with that baby in harvest?"

Mama said, "Same thing as if she was my real baby, take her with me."

After the friend left, Mama really thought, "What *am* I going to do with a baby?!"

Mama always said she thought she heard a voice saying, "What would you do with one of your own?"

And she replied, "Well, Lord, I would have to do the best I could."

She always said, "I just went and got the other two, but the Lord meant for me to raise Jean."

Mama Emma and Daddy Jimmy were sharecroppers on Mr. George Posey's plantation. We lived on the plantation at a place called Gahagan outside of Coushatta from 1951 to 1960.

Jimmy King was very religious. We were not allowed to play cards or jacks in the house. When the spirituals went off, we had to turn off the radio. He would come in and fuss at mama and I for listening to the *Louisiana Hayride* on Saturday night before going to church. He said all that was the devil's work. Daddy did not drink coffee in the morning. He would just heat water and drink it with sugar. Daddy mainly read his Bible and other books he had in his room; he was a quiet man. He was about 5'8" tall and weighed about 150 lbs.

He was always trying to keep me from getting a whooping. He would tell me, "Don't get in a storm while I'm gone."

Somehow, I would always manage to catch a whooping when he was gone. I think he only whooped me once or twice; he was rougher on the boys.

Emma King was also religious; however, she was worldlier than Daddy when it came to entertainment. Mama Emma was 5'10" and weighed about 220 lbs. She loved to drink her coffee every morning, sometimes with a lil' nip of whiskey if anyone brought any to the

## I. FROM THE PLANTATION TO THE HILL

house. Mama was good at cooking. She made good homemade teacakes, sweet potato pies, and fried chicken. She had a laugh out of this world and always did a "belly laugh," as we would say. She didn't take any mess. If you wanted to show out, she would right along with you, no matter the place. Mama did all the whipping; she was good but firm.

I participated in the sharecropping work on the plantation once I was old enough.

We would plant Mr. Posey's cotton and hoe it. Cotton was the main crop. We would get our share of money from the crop, and he would get his. We had other crops like peas, corn, tomatoes, peanuts, potatoes, okra and much more. These were crops for our eating and survival. We would take the corn to the mill to grind it into cornmeal. We made our own bread; most of the time, we had cornbread. That went well with collard or mustard greens.

We planted in late January or February and harvested in late November. When harvest time came and the cotton bolls opened, I was allowed to pick it.

When Mr. Posey sold his cotton crops, he gave my family a share in it and to those who stayed on the plantation. During those years, he had a little plantation store where you could get things on the book, but we never did.

My dad would tell us, "Don't fool with it."

If you bought something from the store on the book, they took it out of your crop money at the end of the year. A lot of people would come out behind, which meant they owed the plantation owner more than they got paid from their share of the crop. So, they had to make up the difference out of their own pockets. If they kept that up, they started the next plantation season in the hole.

Mama and Daddy would struggle to do without. They sacrificed and made do until the end of the year. Whatever money we cleared, Mr. George shared with us. Then, we used that money to buy whatever we wanted.

One thing that can ruin a harvest is coming out behind. Thank God when we were farming and sharecropping, we never came out behind. For us, there was never a tense moment looking at the book.

Daddy could read and write; he kept a record for himself. Daddy always signed his name as Jimmy King. They wanted him to make an "X," but he did not want

## I. FROM THE PLANTATION TO THE HILL

to make one. He knew his handwriting; no one could fake his writing and pretend he put an X when he did not. Most of the others on the plantation signed with an X to identify themselves. Daddy would never get anything on credit. If you were unable to sacrifice and constantly going to buy clothes and junk, harvest could be more stressful. Daddy kept things orderly and simple.

We raised our own cows, hogs, chickens and mules; no horses by my time. The mules were used to plow the field.

A normal day in the fields would begin with us finishing breakfast by 7 AM. We always got to the field no later than 8 AM. You could not hoe cotton while the dew was on the ground. We had to wait for the sun to get up and dry the dew. If anyone wanted water, I could bring them water and stuff like that. We would stay out there from 8 AM until 6 PM. A lot of times, we left food on the stove cooking on the back burner. We would break for lunch at noon. Sometimes we would stay out in the fields and just go under the tree to eat lunch.

Hoeing cotton was not easy work, and my vision problem only made it more challenging. I once chopped a whole row of cotton down by mistake; after that, I was told to stay under the shade tree while the cotton was being chopped. My vision was not good enough to know where the cotton ended and the grass began.

It was at this time that the first surgery I had in Shreveport failed. The doctors discovered I had cataracts in my eyes. I always wondered why they would mess with my eyes. My foster parents knew I could see birds in the trees before the surgery.

After age 5, I noticed I could not see as well as before. Having the surgery at age 5 delayed me from starting school. The adults said they wanted my eyes to adjust to the surgery.

At age 7, I went to the health unit. My foster dad was writing and signing me up for shots. He was the only person in the house who could read and write. He had an eighth-grade education. Mama never went to school, but she had a lot of what she called "mother wit."

While we were at the health unit, I wanted to sign up my dolls. I got the papers and held the tablet close to my face. They realized then that the surgery was not successful.

## I. FROM THE PLANTATION TO THE HILL

So, I was told about the school for the blind. When I first started going to the school for the blind, Daddy used to come and get me on the train, and we would come back together. This went on until I learned to travel independently about a year after starting school by traveling with the other blind student.

Being blind did not stop me from having chores. I had responsibilities like everyone else. We did not have electricity in the home, so we used kerosene lamps. It was my job every morning to blow out the lamps, take out the chamber pots, wash them and leave them outside in the sun until night time. It was my job to bring them back inside and place them by the beds, too. I also had to bring in wood for the stove. I was too little to bring in logs for the fireplace, but I could bring in arms full of wood for the stove. I was not allowed to light the lamp because that was "fooling with fire."

Once I went to school and Mama saw what all the other blind children could do, I got more responsibilities. Then I had to add more chores to my list, including ironing, washing dishes, and sweeping.

When I swept and mopped, I would clean while barefoot to evaluate the floors as I worked. I learned to use my fingertips to check for wrinkles as I ironed.

When I washed dishes, I would rub my fingertips to hear the squeak of clean dishes.

Most days on the plantation were uneventful. The most eventful days on Posey's plantation were hog killing day, listening to the radio, coming home from school in Baton Rouge, Christmas, and church.

In the winter, it was really cold on the plantation. A lot of times, we had to stuff rags into the holes in the floor to stay warm. We had only one room with a fireplace. In the kitchen, the water we used for drinking would freeze in the buckets. That's how our house was, COLD! There was no heat if we did not light a fire.

We used to kill hogs on the first cold day after Christmas. Sometimes that day was in mid-January. Daddy always went by if it was clear and cold the night before; then, the next day might be a hog killing day. Ideally, we wanted the temperature to be between 35 degrees to 45 degrees, no more than 55 degrees. While the butchering occurs, you don't want it to be beyond 55 degrees outside or the meat could spoil.

Some people would stab the hog and then slice its throat. My dad would shoot the hog in the head and then pour extremely hot water on the hide to get all the hair off. Afterwards, we bled it out, cut it open, and

## I. FROM THE PLANTATION TO THE HILL

took the intestines where we could wash them. That would be your chitlins. We would take out the different parts and cut them as we wanted, usually sausage and hog head cheese. I would run around and help do whatever I could.

One thing I enjoyed was playing with the blowout, which was the hog's bladder. It was shaped like a balloon and had air in both ends. Another thing I enjoyed was people coming from other plantations to help with cutting, curing, and packaging the meat.

At the end of the day, it was sharing time. Anyone who participated would get a piece of hog to take home, so they could have fresh meat for the winter. Without refrigeration, we would put the meat in the smokehouse or a big ol' barrel with tons of salt to cure it. All of this would happen between November to mid-February.

When we kept our cured meat too long in the summertime, it would be kind of rancid. You could smell it. Now that I think about it, it smelled like an unwashed vagina during a menstrual cycle. It was called tainted meat, but we still ate it. We would fry or boil it. We also bred our hogs. If we had a good bow or sail, they made good shoat for eating.

As a child, I had a problem with worms a couple of times. The worms would crawl around in my nose, and Mama would see them in my stool. She addressed them by giving me her *"concoction."* I believe it was made of sulfur, honey, and garlic with a little turpentine. Later, I would throw up and worms were crawling in the lard bucket we used. Mama's remedy for worms worked. After that, Mama and Daddy started closely watching my time outside, specifically in the chicken yard and with hogs and cows. We also had 14 dogs and 14 cats. My favorite dog was named Blacky; she was a German Shepherd.

Once, Mama brought me some wieners and bread in a pan. I would take a bite and then Blacky would. She did not just gobble it up, she ate a little at a time; Mama said we were close.

I was very close to my foster brother, James King Junior. Junior and Bill King were blood brothers, really my distant cousins. Junior was six years older than me and one year older than Bill. I would jump at the chance to show them I was not handicapped. No matter the adventure or dare, I could play however they did.

## I. FROM THE PLANTATION TO THE HILL

Once, my brother Bill said, "Bet you won't burn Daddy's hat!"

Being the spontaneous person I was and looking for acceptance, I said, "Yes I will!"

Bill said, "No, you won't!"

As I reached my arm out, I said, "Give it here!"

Then, I threw the hat in the fireplace. It made a whooshing sound. The orange flames burned so brightly that even I could see them.

Next thing I knew Daddy asked me, "Did you burn my hat?"

Fearfully, I answered, "Yes sir."

Bill had run and told him; Daddy just wanted to confirm his story. I was never good at lying; I only wanted to belong.

After I confessed that I burned his hat, Daddy whooped me. He only whipped me twice in my life, so this was a rare occasion.

I really wanted to be with my blood kin; church time was the most likely time for that. Jerusalem Church was one of four churches we attended occasionally. We had to catch a ride there; it was too far to walk.

My favorite sister, and the one I kind of knew, was Connie. Her foster people belonged to Jerusalem, and my mama would go to that church. Connie and I would find each other. I wanted her to go home with me, and she wanted me to go home with her. We each had our own foster family that we were being raised by. Virginia Grey was raising Connie.

Mama Emma would always say, "Baby girl, here is your sister" while showing me to Connie.

At the time, I did not know I was a foster child. I just knew my people were raising me. No state agent was in charge of me, so I did not consider myself a foster child.

I did not like leaving my sister. I used to live for those times when we went to Jerusalem, on the third Sunday. Seeing her was always good for me. We always cried and had to be physically separated to go home.

I haven't seen Connie since I was 17, and she was 15. She came to tell me goodbye because she was moving to California for good. We kept in contact over

## I. FROM THE PLANTATION TO THE HILL

the years, but Connie passed away before I ever got a chance to see her again.

Maybe twice, I saw Lucy Bell, my real grandmother. She came to church occasionally before moving to California in 1959, roughly 10 years before Connie and her kids moved there. Carrie Lee's younger siblings, Aunt Ruby and Uncle Allen, nicknamed "Snig", would see me as often as possible when we were teenagers. I still contact Uncle Snig; he is not much older than me and always found a way to see about me.

I have crossed paths with Billy, my older brother. He has since passed, but I remain in contact with his wife.

I have always loved church. In fact, Mama said the first time I spoke was not just words. We were in Starlight Baptist Church when I led a solo. There was a group singing named "The William Family." Uninvited and off the program, I went up and sang with them, "I got heaven on my mind." Mama tried to stop me three times.

I enjoyed working in the church. Raising money for the church was important to me. Mama would go around town with me and let me sing. Afterwards, the people would often put money in my envelope for church.

One time we went to a dry-cleaning business for donations. After I sang my solo, there was one particular worker I asked a lot of questions to.

I said, "I bet you don't know my name?"

She replied enthusiastically, "Your name is Sandra Jean!"

I was completely shocked. I said, "Well, I bet you don't know how old I am?"

She said, "You are 5 years old."

I was befuddled. Feeling challenged, I responded, "Well, you sure don't know when my birthday is!"

Without hesitation, she replied, "Your birthday is May 12$^{th}$."

After that, she put money in my envelope. Mama and I went out the door.

I told Mama, "There was a lady that knew all about me. How did that lady know me?"

Mama said, "Baby, that was your real mama, Carrie Lee."

## I. FROM THE PLANTATION TO THE HILL

Confused, I replied, "My real mama?"

At that moment, Carrie Lee came out to us.

Mama said, "Carrie Lee, you oughta be ashamed of yourself! Come see your child sometimes."

Carrie Lee replied, "I will, Cousin Emma" while giving me some nasty candy.

She promised to buy me a walking, talking doll. That was one of two times I saw Carrie Lee, in my whole life. The other time was after my first failed eye surgery. I never got the doll.

The church has always been a go-between for me and my birth family to cross paths. I grew up going to different churches around the community. There were so few people that lived there that some of the same people sang in multiple church choirs.

Starlight Baptist Church was the one my family belonged to, along with Mr. Ed Brock and his family. The Brocks stayed on Mr. Charlie's plantation, which was nearby. The Gate Church was another one we attended; it was really named Mary Magdalene Church. They had New Mary Magdalene and Old Mary Magdalene. Old Mary Magdalene was in a place called Herman, LA; it was not within walking distance.

The Gate Church, Starlight Baptist, and Willard Grove were all right around each other. We would go from church to church. It was one service a month for each church. They could not have church every Sunday because every small church had to have its turn having its services.

I can recall Mr. Ed Brock. He was considered a historical figure in our community. He, and his wife Mrs. Kitty, had a large family. He would be the lead singer, prayer man, etc. at all three churches every Sunday. If he was not allowed to do these things regularly, his mouth would be "poked out a mile," Mama would say.

He had a big bass voice like Melvin aka "Blue" from The Temptations.

No matter who would be praying or doing the service, Mr. Brock would sit with his arms crossed and say, "What a mess."

When it was his turn to lead, you could hear him from miles away singing "Whoa, oh Lordy!" He was around 100 years old then, between 1952 and 1954.

When I was a little girl and it rained really bad, we caught a ride with somebody. We could not get back

## I. FROM THE PLANTATION TO THE HILL

into the plantation because water would be everywhere. There was no concrete. Everybody would take turns carrying me since I was the youngest.

I would get on Mr. Ed's shoulders. He spoke frequently of his time as a slave. He often recalled being sold from North Carolina to Louisiana at the age of 14. He also remembered being scared on the night the stars fell in 1833.

All of us got along like family, from plantation to plantation. Everybody helped everybody with their crop in harvest. Along with the Brock Family on Charlie Stewart's plantation, I got to know the Johnson Family, Ms. Narsis, and her mother, Ms. Ola. Ms. Ola had three other girls, but they were all married and moved away.

Our greatest entertainment was the radio shows like *The Shadow, Gunsmoke, Guiding Light,* and *Our Gal Sunday*. We had to turn the radio on 30 minutes before the program aired. The battery took so long to warm up. It was huge, like a car battery. We did not have television or phones at the time. If there was a fight or ballgame, people would come from all around to hear. Whichever house had a radio was the place to meet. The team I used to listen for was the Houston Colt .45s; they later became the Astros.

People would also come from all around to have Mama make their clothes. When they came for that, I would have to "get somewhere and sit down."

Back then, children were taught to be seen not heard. I would always say something and get in trouble.

Most often, when Mama spoke and said something wrong, I would correct her, "No ma'am, it's so and so…"

I could be sure to get a whipping when the people left.

Sometimes, only the women from the surrounding plantations would come and quilt. They would just sit around, sew patches, and gossip. You could find out a lot of information at a Quilting Bee. That's what they called it; you may know it as "the tea." For example, if an unwed person became pregnant, people would say she "broke a leg" or "got spoiled."

On Sundays, when we came home from church, the preacher or somebody from church would come home with us. Throughout the week, people were busy maintaining their farms. So, usually Sundays were the

## I. FROM THE PLANTATION TO THE HILL

visiting days. Mama would cook food for us and our guests. During those times, the preacher would have his pick of the meat, and the children ate what was left. But not in our household. Mama and Daddy believed that children should eat the same as everyone else.

A lot of times, I would ask Daddy, "Can I eat out of your plate?"

I knew he would leave me something to eat.

"Y'all gon' be here long after the preacher," he would say. "The world was rolling before you got here; it is going to roll when you leave."

That meant having reverence for other people. Don't think the world revolves around you.

Mama Emma had a lot of rules. One was if you did not have enough to share, don't bring it out amongst company. Of course, I did not follow that.

Once, I asked for some cake in front of a bunch of children. Mama had already told me we did not have enough cake to share. Since it was not enough, Mama gave the children the cake, and I didn't get any.

Mama also taught us not to lie or steal. Ask somebody, don't take it. These were hard lessons, but I knew Mama Emma loved me, even though there were times she would get mad at Daddy and say, "None of these bastards are kin to me! I did not have to raise them." She was referring to me and my foster brothers.

On Saturdays, Daddy would take me to make groceries. My mom rarely went to the grocery store; Dad went mostly because it was along the walk home from the highway. A car could not get all the way up where we stayed, deep in the fields.

Sometimes along the way, Daddy would drop me off at my relatives' house, too. He would take me to my Aunt Crecy's home; it gave me a chance to get to know them while he shopped. Aunt Crecy was Lucy Bell's sister, my great-aunt.

One time, while her children and I were playing, she called them inside, one by one. Each child was inside for about 15 minutes or more and then came back outside chewing. I could smell onions and gravy.

I asked, "What y'all eating?"

"Steak and gravy," she answered.

Things like this went on with that part of the family often.

## I. FROM THE PLANTATION TO THE HILL

I told Daddy I was hungry when he came back.

"They didn't give you anything?!" he asked.

After that, Daddy never left me with them again. 'Til this day, I still don't like steak and gravy.

Before that, I was visiting the same aunt's house and they had something I love, watermelon. They had cut the watermelon in quarter spears for everybody to eat.

A woman asked, "Anybody want more?"

Everyone threw their melon rinds away, including me. They took my hands, wiped them off, and told me to go sit down, but they gave all the other children a second serving.

When I became grown, that same aunt would come over to Mama's house and try to find me, whenever I came from Baton Rouge to visit. By that time, I did not care about those incidents anymore.

A time of year I really loved was Christmas. I would come home from school in December around the 17th for Christmas break.

At church, we would have a Christmas program on Christmas Day. I could learn my part in a week if I had something to say in person and also learn my brother Junior's part. He was always slower, but he was my favorite brother. I could not stand to see him struggle to remember his part in the program. So, when he would forget, I would whisper his part to him.

We had a tradition back home. First, we had a prayer meeting in the house. Afterwards, we would look in a big 'ol box. The gifts would not be wrapped; they were just sitting there waiting for us.

We would then attend church. If someone came up to you and yelled "Christmas gift," you had to give away something right there on the spot. Later, I learned this traditional game came from England. The best gift I got for Christmas was money; the worst was a slice of Juicy Fruit gum.

Another major holiday for us was the 19th of June, now known as Juneteenth. We never celebrated the 4th of July because that was considered White folks' day. We ate good food, including my favorites, fried chicken and watermelon. We didn't have to go to the field because it was "Lay By Time," which was leaving a crop to mature after hoeing for a final time.

A lot of our traditions and ways followed us when we left the plantation. My family had already moved to

## I. FROM THE PLANTATION TO THE HILL

Couchanda Hill while I was in school; we moved in the spring of 1960. We settled in our crop in the fall of 1959 and got $1,300. I remember that was "big time" back then.

I came home for Christmas just a little bit before we moved. We went on the bus to Shreveport to visit some relatives.

I got on the bus and announced, "We gon' get a new house, and we got $1,300 from our crops!"

Frightened and furious, Mama said, "Someone is going to come on here and kill us, girl! Telling all our business!"

Our new house in Coushatta was an old-time home from 1906. It was a big two-story house that was too big to load up and put on the bridge. They had to tear the house down and rebuild it on Couchanda Hill; it was west of Highway 1. They had so much lumber leftover that they built other things like a smokehouse, crib and wash house, along with the big house. A lot of Blacks were buying houses out there at this time.

Twenty to thirty years after we moved, they discovered coal under the property.

I moved there in May after I got out of school.

I asked Daddy, "What color is our house?"

He said, "It is all kinds of colors. They haven't painted it yet."

There were no electrical codes, so whoever knew how to wire a house did so, same for the buildings. The only thing we did not have was plumbing in the house, but no one else had plumbing either.

It was a 9-bedroom house with a big back porch. The nine rooms were for my daddy to help people who had been flooded. The Great Flood of 1927 caused local waterways to overflow in north Louisiana. People were leery about floods. We had enough rooms just in case someone came to stay with us.

This house was so much bigger than the house we stayed in on the plantation; I thought I might get lost in it. We only had a wooden stove on the plantation, but on the hill we had electricity, a gas stove, and a butane tank.

Without plumbing, we usually just washed off. Taking baths was for when the weather warmed up or on the weekend because we had to get water from a spring down under the hill. On rainy days, we used

## I. FROM THE PLANTATION TO THE HILL

water off the roof that we collected in barrels. We didn't get plumbing until the '70s.

Ms. Charity Russell, along with a few other families, lived on this hill. Once we bought our property, we did not do cotton or have cows anymore. Our focus was on chickens and hogs. Ms. Russell was friends with my family.

One day in the field, they were picking cotton by the day ,and a bumble bee got in Ms. Russell's underwear. Back then, underwear was more like long shorts called "step-ins" with rubber at the bottom.

The bee got in and she ran to my daddy, "Deacon Jimmy, get this bee out of my draws!"

My daddy hollered out to Mama, "Come here, girl! Help get her out of here!"

Everybody in the field laughed.

At night, when we first moved to Couchanda Hill, the woods near our homes would "mysteriously" catch on fire. The flames would burn almost every night.

Daddy and other men in the area formed a watch group, known today as Neighborhood Watch. Deacon Johnson, his boys, Deacon Wilson, his children, the

Green family, and many other people joined. Some of them stayed across the river in Shreveport and Mansfield; they easily had 100 people ready. They would stay up all night and be on the lookout while the women and children slept.

Often the grown-ups would joke and say, "You can pee more water than the Coushatta Fire Department had water."

The fires had us scared to sleep. There were no streetlights, and it was dark. All we had was moonlight and the stars.

Soon after the watch group started, the fires stopped. I guess whoever started these fires respected, feared, or was surprised by our armed men in the woods at night.

One day Daddy and some of the other men were walking in the woods and found gas oil cans. We knew the fires were not random with evidence of an arsonist.

We had other troubles on the hill. My brother Bill had an altercation with a White man. He slapped him over his paycheck. The man did not pay Bill for hauling and making bales of hay. The man said he didn't owe Bill any money because Bill didn't come to work.

## I. FROM THE PLANTATION TO THE HILL

The man came to my daddy about it because he was respected in the community. Daddy was ordered that Bill had to leave town that very day; if not, Bill would be in trouble. Daddy got the money together and put Bill on the first bus out of town.

We woke up the next morning with a cross sitting in the yard out front. It was not burnt, but it was still out there.

Another time, during the summer, a cross was burned in front of Starlight Baptist Church. I think it was because Black people were going to the church to register to vote. The police had heard about it, and they came over and pretended to be concerned about the burning.

They said, "Anything we could do for y'all, let us know."

All of us thought it was probably them that burned it.

Back then, White folks openly demonstrated a lack of tolerance for Blacks. During one of my doctor's appointments in Shreveport, we went to a store nearby that had a lunch counter. As Black people, we could not eat at the counter, so we often waited outside.

There was a mechanical horse for little children to ride. It cost a dime.

At this point, I could see people, clothes, and hair color but not facial reactions. There was a girl there with long blonde hair down to her waist having a terrific time on the horse. When her dime ran out, I jumped on the horse.

My mama yelled, "Jean, get down!"

I said enthusiastically, "Put your money in!" as I bounced up and down.

A guy who worked there came out of the store and said, "Get her off the horse! Get the nigger off the horse!"

My mama dragged me off the horse. I was kicking and crying. I wanted to play like the other girl, and that was very upsetting to me.

One summer break, I went back home from the blind school. Mama and I caught the bus to Shreveport. No matter how many empty seats were in the front, we had to go to the back, if we were lucky enough to even have a seat.

## I. FROM THE PLANTATION TO THE HILL

On this trip, the bus was filled. We passed by many White people in the front, and they would lean away from us as we walked by; all on the window like we stank. When I was almost to the back, I reached my hand out to see if anyone or anything was there. As I did, sounds of disgust erupted.

"Well, I never! That nigger slapped me!"

I did not try to, but I accidentally hit her glasses while they were on her face while I was reaching for the back of the seat.

Mama apologized profusely, "Sorry, she got bad eyes. She did not mean to do it. I'm taking her to the doctor now."

I slapped that woman, and I'm glad I did, acting like we were contagious. I wish I could have slapped her over and over again, but Mama would have had a heart attack, stroke, and everything else!

From the plantation to the hill were turbulent times; however, we always managed to enjoy each other through fellowship. Although I would only come home twice a year, during Christmas and summer, I was never a stranger between letters, visits, and gifts. I always knew how much my family loved me.

# Chapter II

## School for the Blind

I must say going to school was kind of new for me and exciting. However, my mother wasn't comfortable with me going to school so far away. She did not want me out of her sight. She felt she would not be able to protect me like she wanted to with me 200 miles away in Baton Rouge. Nobody was "gon' see after her Jean," as she would say.

After it was determined that my surgery failed, I had to go down to Baton Rouge. At that time, there was no special education for blind people in Red River Parish. So, I started school at the Louisiana State School for Blind Negros at Southern University in September 1957. I was seven years old.

The best thing about my school was meeting my husband and learning how to be self-sufficient; this stands out to me.

Once, while back home on a school vacation, I was trying to see the wrinkles in my clothes and burned my lip. That's when I realized my second surgery failed.

That was one of my major steps to learning how to do things without any kind of sight. I do know and will say, "It don't take eyes for everything."

There were two schools for the blind. One was on Government Street for the White blind children. The one on Southern University's campus was for the Black blind children. Everybody at the school was not totally blind.

It was my understanding that Mrs. Theus, who was my principal then, went to the president of Southern University, Dr. Samuel Clark, and asked if they could have a little spot on their property for the blind Negro children because they had nowhere to go. They were not admitted at the state school for the blind on Government Street. So, they granted Mrs. Theus her request.

I think the first student to go to that school was Phillip Richard. I did not know him, but the school was founded in 1922. That is the historical beginning of the school for the blind at Southern University.

I was never a shy or a quiet person. I have always loved to sing. I sang at church in Coushatta, and I brought my singing down to Baton Rouge with me.

## II. SCHOOL FOR THE BLIND

After they dropped me off, my mom and them tried to tell me bye before they left. I was walking around talking to all the children.

I said, "Hey! What's your name? My name is Sandra Jean Cole! What's your name?" I wanted to know everyone's name. "You going to this school?! I'm going to this school!"

At the school, we had something called chapel every Wednesday from 2 PM to 3 PM in the auditorium. It was like a talent show. We had talented speakers, poets, and singers.

On the first Wednesday in September, I went on stage and sang a gospel song named, "Ima Make It Somehow." I had the whole auditorium rockin'!

Afterwards, we laughed and said I must have thought I was in church.

But as a whole, I did not like the school. I was used to getting my way at home and living with fewer people.

In my dorm, it was six of us in a ward. They called our rooms wards. I was accustomed to sleeping in bed while eating wieners.

I would cry out, "I want to eat wieners! I want to go home! I want my mama!"

But we were not allowed to eat any more food until 7 AM in the morning. If we were hungry after 5 PM, too bad. I always thought that was cruel. We had no snacks and stayed in our dorms. I expected to have my favorite foods at my disposal. It was very disappointing when I did not have them.

Our housemother worked seven days a week and stayed on campus. A lot of us stayed on campus, too. We needed money if we wanted to go home. My parents did not have money to send for me. So for a long time, I only went home twice a year, usually during the summer and Christmas. Anytime I went home was on public transportation. At the time, it was a train called Kansas City Southern. The train went from New Orleans to Kansas City, and between these stops was Coushatta.

A lot of times, the housemother would designate older girls to take charge of us. I was assigned a girl to comb my hair and help me dress. I could dress myself but not pick out my clothes. That went on until I was allowed to do it for myself.

## II. SCHOOL FOR THE BLIND

As a child, I was lonesome. I knew I would meet some children to play with at the school. They had a lot of children to play with. The other children and classes were just down the walkway from my dorm. We went to school from 8 AM to 3 PM and had breakfast at 7 AM. After we came back from breakfast, the big girl in charge would make sure that we were ready for school.

One thing I liked about the school was that they had electricity and indoor plumbing. Back home, we did not have any of that. I was amazed with the lights on the wall. You would flip a switch and the light would come on. Sometimes I just flicked it up and down to hear it go, "click, click, click." It was fascinating to me.

I went back home and told my daddy I wanted some lights. He actually put in electricity and bought a refrigerator. Before that, the ice man would come once a week to bring us blocks of ice to keep our milk and butter cool in our icebox. I was tired of lamps.

The time at home always flew by. Back at school, I would miss my mom petting me up. But they had this one girl named Bercy that would sometimes let me get in bed with her and lay down if I cried at night for my mom. As an older girl, I got to be on the cheerleader team, in the choir, took piano, and gave a couple of recitals. I did not like playing music and reading braille music sheets; it was hard. So, I had to memorize my music.

When it came to food, I thought the school could do better, especially when I saw the grown-ups working there taking the food home. The principal would be in another room eating a different kind of food, like steak and ground meat, while we ate the cast-off food. The food at the school could be horrible. I noticed the food was better on special days like Sunday dinner or on parent's day in May at the end of the school year.

Whenever they thought a parent was coming, they had cake, chicken, rice and gravy. That was fancy food. More often through the week, they had what I called slop.

One morning, sardines and grits were our breakfast. For supper, we had tuna fish with one peach and a slice of bread. On Sundays, we never had dinner, only breakfast and lunch. If we had food after lunch, it would be a peanut butter and jelly or a meat sandwich, an apple or orange, and a slice of cake. Some students thought that was enough.

## II. SCHOOL FOR THE BLIND

The only time we were allowed to have something after our meal was when we got on the big girls' end. That was when we could afford to order from the local businesses, and the delivery man would come and bring our food. But as a little girl, I could not order.

There were some girls on the big girl end that took a liking to me. Most of the girls did not like me. They said I was "fast" and "smart mouth." I did not care about what they said. However, I could always run to Jennie, Bertha, and Bercy.

One day, a little girl who was soon to be my roommate begged me, "Sandy! Sandy, let's play fighting!"

I did not see the sense in play fighting. If you are going to fight, then fight. If you are not going to fight, then don't start hitting each other.

But she kept saying, "Sandy, come on! Let's play fighting."

I was like, "I don't really want to fight. Come on! Let's fight!"

With that invitation, she hit me on my left shoulder with an open palm. I was in the game now! I quickly grabbed her knee and ankle. I bent them behind her back until she fell.

Once her knee hit the concrete floor she screamed out, "Owl! Sandy, my leg!" Soon after that she was crying.

I was a little shocked. I thought, Why is she screaming when she was the one that wanted to play fighting?

When she screamed, the people down the hall came running to see what was going on. It was a bunch of people that were bigger than I was. They nearly surrounded me. While entering the room, they asked "What's going on? What's happening in here?"

Then that little girl said, "Sandy hit my leg on the floor."

While the big girls were checking the girl's injury, I was inching toward the wall. Different members of that crowd were saying, "I knew it, you were always so mean, so fast and so loud! I know you did it! You so fast. Now we going to take your leg and hit it on the floor."

The mob yelled, "Let's get her!"

## II. SCHOOL FOR THE BLIND

By the time they came for me, I made it to the door. I knew I could not fight them all. So, I ran down the hall onto the big girl's end of the dorm. I could see enough not to run into anything. I ran out of my shoes.

A girl named Jennie came out of her room and asked me, "Why are you running? Where are you going, Sandy?"

Scared and crying I said, "Them children trying to beat me up. I ain't got no friends."

Jennie said, "Come on in here."

Then, she picked me up and went in the room. Bertha was in there. Jennie sat down with me on her lap.

I said, "They don't like me and don't want to be my friend."

Bertha and Jennie said, "We will be your friends."

Bertha and Jennie were true to their word. They were like my guardian angels.

As I got older, I was assigned to dress a little girl named Margie May. She had seizures and was nonverbal. I bathed her, dressed her, combed her hair, and brushed her teeth. She would throw things at me and anybody else while calling us all kinds of names. Somehow, I had the patience to fool with her. I was 15 years old dressing 10-year-old Margie May. She was a big girl for her age. I was short. She was taller than me, which was challenging.

The older I got, the more fun I had. On Friday nights, we had a dance called a social, where the boys and girls dance and had fun together. Walking back from the dance, if you had a boyfriend, you might kiss him on the way back if you found a dark spot or low light area.

In 1965, Sam Cooke had a song called "Shake." I got on the floor as he sang, "shake it like a bowl of soup; make your body go loop-de-loop." We liked to dance like everybody else. Also, there was a dance my principal called "rotten," and we called it "The Dog!" We also did The Philly Dog, Shimmy, Shake, and Twist.

Sometimes, we had a movie to watch on Saturday nights in the auditorium. On Sunday mornings, we always went to different churches. A bus would pick us up and bring us back.

When I was 15 years or older, there was something called "open campus." That's when I saw

## II. SCHOOL FOR THE BLIND

my boyfriend once a week, between 2 PM and 5 PM on Sundays. All my boyfriends did not go to the school for the blind. Two of my boyfriends were related to my friend Loretta. I would see them sometimes at Loretta's house. I did not date boys for long. Usually after a week, I'd date another boy. Terry was the last boy that came to the school that I dated for a long time. That was my best time, outside with the boys. If I did something bad, my housemother would take away my open campus privilege. Ms. Satler, one of our housemothers, would use cleaning for punishment. My friend Teretha, who had no boyfriend often received this punishment. I would have mopped 10 hallways and 15 rooms to not miss open campus.

Girls from the School for Deaf Negros, next door to us, would do our hair. It seemed like the deaf girls thought they were better than us because we were blind. We paid a quarter to get our hair done. They would come running up behind us making these strange noises to get their money sometimes. These girls always wanted to come over and try to make fun of us and belittle us because they were doing our hair. I hurried up and learned how to do my own hair, so they would not have to do mine. I burned it a couple of times, but I did it anyway.

To this day, I feel a certain way. It always looks like to me, society gives them more leeway to shine then they give the blind.

I disliked Saturdays in the daytime. It was always boring. We had to clean, mop, and count the linen. We did not have a maid.

In later years, I found out that the White school had maids. We had to count the sheets, take them outside to the laundry, and bring them back to the dorm when they were finished. There was this one girl, Patricia, who peed in the bed. Everyone hated counting sheets when she did that.

We did not have anything done for us. I did not like all that counting linen and mopping. I felt like we should not have had to do all that, but it made me more efficient and taught me how to do for myself.

I also learned to read recipes, cook, and sew. We learned how to sew clothes, hem, and put on buttons with a machine. All of this was a part of my stay from 1957 to 1969.

In 1965, Hurricane Betsy hit. I was at the school in Baton Rouge. During this hurricane, a chlorine barge sunk in the Mississippi River. About a month after

## II. SCHOOL FOR THE BLIND

that, they were going to raise it up. Everybody in Baton Rouge had to leave because they did not know if the fumes would be deadly.

Going to a resident school, we could not just go home 200 miles away and come back on a bus in one day. So, the school gave us a week off. My dad told me since we had this big ol' house, if I had some school friends, bring them with me if they were from Baton Rouge. My friend Loretta came home with me. We stayed that week in Coushatta. The barge was lifted without incident.

By inviting Loretta to my house, I ended up getting invited to her house on the weekends. I did not have to stay at the school all the time after that. My mom and dad signed a permission slip that allowed me to go to Loretta's house. Now on Easter or Thanksgiving, I did not have to stay at the school.

I remember during this period between 1957 and 1959, while I was at the resident school, my foster brother, Junior, had gotten a car.

My parents wrote a letter, "Dear Jean, your brother will come and get you for Christmas. You don't have to ride the train."

I was so excited. Since my brother got a car in October, it would be only a couple of months before he would come and pick me up for Christmas. I was proud and happy.

I told the other children, "I don't have to ride that nasty, stinky train like y'all do. My brother coming to get me! Y'all 'blinies' gon' be on the train, but I won't be. I'll be in a car."

About a week later, my parents wrote me, "Dear Jean, your brother will not be able to come get you because he wrecked his car and totaled it."

I later learned he was driving out in the fields showing off, going 90 miles an hour. Daddy had paid $500 cash for the car. Five hundred dollars was a lot of money at that time. I put a good face on, but I ended up on the train.

The following May, my dad came to my eighth-grade graduation.

He said, "You done good! I'm proud of you."

I said, "That ain't nothing Dad, wait 'til I put on that cap and gown in '69."

Dad said, "Oh, I won't be around for that."

## II. SCHOOL FOR THE BLIND

Sure enough, he was not. He passed away in 1966 with stomach cancer. On his deathbed, Dad wanted me to promise to finish high school and marry one of the boys from my school. I promised to do both to ease his mind.

After Daddy died, I met Terry Trotter, my two older children's father. We met when I was in tenth grade. He graduated in 1967, two years before me. He could not read the writing on the board from the back of the room in public school. He was what we called visually impaired.

He was a shy boy, and I was the kind of person that would try to bring out your shyness. When I found out he was the new boy on campus, I made a vow. I was gon' get that new boy.

He played on the basketball team, and we played other schools. People did not like when we beat them. Often the official and other teams would cheat to keep us from beating them.

One time after we won, Terry asked me to go out with him to celebrate. He was too shy to wait around for my answer.

He said, "Girl, you want to go to the BBQ?" Then, he walked away.

To myself I was like, "I'm going with this boy because he is a new boy, and he nice looking, so they tell me." Anytime a new boy would come to the school, girls with some vision would describe how he looked to the girls without any vision.

While Terry was on the basketball team, I was a cheerleader. We played and beat Dorceyville High School. It was a school right down the road from Plaquemine, Louisiana, by the Mississippi River.

The referee was fussing at the Dorceyville players saying, "How y'all let a bunch of blind people beat y'all?!"

We played Brusly High school, too. I was jumping up and down cheering while they were playing ball. When the boys played basketball, Mary, Martha, and I were the main cheerleaders. Mary and Martha were twins. There were five of us in total. The five of us wore red shirts and white blouses as we shouted, "Go! Go! Go! Go! The mighty tigers!"

Every time our team would score a point, we would jump up, shake our hips, and do a little two-step

## II. SCHOOL FOR THE BLIND

dance. The sighted people at public school games were surprised blind people could dance and even more surprised when we won the games. It was really nice to participate and be a part of a so-called normal high school experience.

I liked to participate in the LIALO rallies. LIALO stood for Louisiana Interscholastic and Literary Association. LIALO was established in 1935 by William Gray of Southern University to provide an organization for the African American students of the state.

We used to participate with regular schools such as Scotlandville High School, McKinley High School, and Capital High School. There were musical and academic competitions. Sometimes, five different schools would sing the same song. A panel of judges from the school system had to see which one sang the best. The judges gave a score ranging from Superior (being the highest), Excellent, Good, Average, and Below Average. Our school always received a Superior score. Also, I received Superior while singing solos. I didn't enroll in science or mathematics competitions because I did not like science and I was not good in mathematics. However, people that went to my school scored high in those subjects. Once all the schools became integrated, these rallies stopped.

I graduated from the Louisiana State School for Blind Negros at Southern University as valedictorian in May 1969. Terry and I got married June 21, 1969.

I don't know if I married Terry out of love. However, I did not want to go back to the country. I was sick of living in the woods. Mama was disappointed. She thought I was gonna go straight back home, and we would be enjoying each other as usual.

I told her, "No Mama, I'm gonna get married. We gon' pick out our furniture, and I'm not coming back."

Terry asked me to marry him, so I did. First, I had to go home to get mama to sign my license because at the time I had to be 21 years of age, and I was only 19 years old.

Then, the next issue was my adoption was not official.

The Clerk of Court asked Mama, "Where is the paperwork of adoption?"

Mama stated, "I don't have any. I raised Jean from 7 months old."

## II. SCHOOL FOR THE BLIND

The Clerk of Court stated, "Well then, you have to go find her mother."

Mama replied, "Well, I don't know where to find her at this time."

The Clerk of Court said, "Hold on. You said you raised her from 7 months old? Now, she's 19 years old? Well, if you don't know if she's ready for marriage, no one else will! Sign these papers!"

But then we had another problem. My birth certificate had me listed as a boy! I did not know that all those years. At that time, it was against the law for people of the same sex to marry in Louisiana. I didn't know I was a boy! There I was looking all fine like a woman but listed as a boy. I had to go back to the school in Baton Rouge for my medical records to prove I was female. Until this day, on my birth certificate, there is a scratch-off where they had me as male, from changes made in June 1969.

# Chapter III
## Southern University

The schools for the blind merged in 1979. I was not a part of the integration because I graduated grade school in 1969. I went to the school from 1957 through 1969, first through twelfth grade, on Southern University's campus.

Many people thought I was in college while I was at the school for the blind. After I started college, they would ask, "Are you still there?!"

After I got married, I decided to take Dictaphone typing. Once I got pregnant, my vocational rehab counselor was mad at me and would not help me pursue my career. He thought I should be a housewife and needed to stay in one area. I was not contented with this.

Mr. Tinney, my counselor, said to me, "Oh well, now that you got a child, you can't work."

At that time, there were not as many computers. It was manual typewriters. By me not typing, my speed went down. I could type 60 words per minute then.

Mr. Tinney said nobody would want me because my typing speed was too slow. He then closed my case.

I stayed home and was a housewife. I took care of my family, cleaned my house, and whatever else. I did not think about going to school anymore until 1975.

Before then, I got in a band on weekends to make extra money; I was the female vocalist. The band was called Black Gold, and there were 10 members. There was a guy that worked for the post office named Dorsey. He was the manager, and he also played horns, drums, and bass. Knighten was the male vocalist. They interacted with me the most. The others played instruments. Our practice was at 10 PM. We had a couple of gigs. My brother Junior came down to see me. He and Terry came to the gigs. The gigs often started at midnight and went until 2 AM or 3 AM.

One thing I did not like about the band was splitting up $150 with nine people. Another thing, the next day, I might want to sleep in, and my little girl would wake up early, hungry. So, I would have to cook breakfast. Being in a band and on the road was not going to work. I knew there must be some other ways to make money.

## III. SOUTHERN UNIVERSITY

First, I began to work on my mobility. My path to my guide dog, Kristi, started at a National Federation of the Blind meeting. A guide dog representative from Guiding Eyes for the Blind in New York came to talk to us about guide dog travel. Terry and I talked it over. We thought it would be safer if I walked around with a guide dog instead of a cane. He suggested that I might want to travel to New York and get the dog because travel and food were free, and it was just three weeks. Also, we did not have to pay for the dog. However, if we wanted to contribute, our donation would be welcomed.

I went in the summer of 1971. I learned that the 4-H Club raised the dogs from puppies. The school was very picky about who the dogs went home with. Kristi had very soft feelings, and did not like a harsh master. The school tried to match the person's personality with the dog's personality. Kristi had two other masters before me. They just did not work out.

Kristi and I hit it off from the start. The school observed us for 24 hours before we got a dog. The class was full of women. It was 13 of us at a school in Peekskill, New York. The next day, they decided to give me Kristi because they thought I was a soft, easygoing, sunny personality type.

When we first got our dogs, it was exciting. The dogs went everywhere with us, including the bathroom. They needed to get used to us giving them commands. They already understood sit, stay, and fetch.

Every night, we did obedience exercises to keep them sharp. All the dogs were Retrievers. The school stopped using German Shepherds because they were too aggressive when people got too close or tried to help their masters.

For the first two and a half weeks of dog training, we traveled in Peekskill, New York. Then we went to White Plains, New York. We learned it was called city travel when sidewalks were available. It was called country or rural travel if there were no sidewalks.

After that, we went to New York City for a day, and we boarded the subways. I was amazed. The subways never stopped, they just slowed down. Kristi knew how to jump on and when the doors opened, she knew how to jump off. You better hold that harness and keep up! It was nice.

## III. SOUTHERN UNIVERSITY

We stayed 26 days total. I went on August 7, 1971 and returned September 1, 1971. I could not wait to get back home. I was so afraid my daughter, Terrlyn, was going to start walking before I got back, but she did not. My route to Guiding Eyes was from Baton Rouge to New Orleans to New York LaGuardia Airport.

On my return, while over Virginia, the plane started going like a Ferris wheel!

I said, "Oh Lord! If you let me out of this plane, I will never get in another." And I have not.

When I got to New Orleans, I caught the bus and came on back to Baton Rouge with Kristi. I had Kristi for about 12 years before she got sick.

Getting around was easier with Kristi, my guide dog. She helped me a lot going back and forth. In the summer of 1973, I went back to the school for the blind at Southern as a teacher's aide. The teacher I was under, Ms. Wallace, did not want to do anything. She wanted me to do all the work and get paid like an aide. Right then and there, I thought if I ever became a teacher, I would know how to treat my aide.

When Ms. Wallace would get mad at me because I did not want to teach her whole class, she would throw in my face, "You better be glad we hired you at the blind school."

My oldest child started school in 1975. I felt I could do more with my life, and I wanted to do more. I went to vocational rehab again and asked them to pay for my tuition for college. There were different counselors, but they had the same thoughts and words as Mr. Tinney.

They said I did not need to go to college because I was already a housewife.

I told them, "You can work and go to school."

At that time, Louisiana did not have a training school for blind people after high school. So, they wanted me to go to Arkansas to learn how to cook and manage a home.

I said, "Instead of sending me to college for homemaking, send me to college to advance myself! I'm already married with a child."

They were not sure about my abilities.

I exclaimed, "Well, if I go and don't pass, then I'm out!" I kept asking and begging.

## III. SOUTHERN UNIVERSITY

Reluctantly, they told me to prove myself by attending one semester. Needless to say, I made the Dean's list during that first semester, in the spring of 1976. Vocational rehab paid for all my expenses, and I didn't need any loans.

On my first day as a freshman, I went to W.W. Steward Hall, and we toured the building. I had my dog; no one had to hold my hands. The person in front was directing us. I got my schedule for my class.

Once I got home with the schedule, Terry would read it. I would convert it to braille. I would walk down to a building named T.T. Alane for math and psychology. Class was on Monday, Wednesday, and Friday; it lasted 55 minutes. On Tuesday and Thursday, I had biology lab and lecture. With my child in school and getting out at 3 PM, I made sure my classes ended at 1 PM. When school was out for the holidays, I brought my 6-year-old daughter to college with me.

I took less hours than the average freshman. I only took 14 hours; a lot of people took 18 hours. I took 14 hours in order to get home and get my daughter Terrlyn off the bus.

Also, I had to have classes that started at 9 AM, so I could be home to put her on the bus in the morning.

Naturally, I wanted to be home to cook supper for my husband. It was challenging.

Then when I became pregnant with my son as a junior in college, I had to walk 3 flights of stairs while heavily pregnant. That became tiresome. Many times, when he was a baby, I'd be so sleepy and put his bottles in the cabinet and the glasses I was washing in the refrigerator.

After I had my son, I did not return to Southern University as a student until January 1980 because the fall semester started when Tyron would have been only a month old. I could not see myself putting my month-old child in the nursery just to go back to school. I waited until he was six months old. Then I went back to school as planned.

I graduated with a bachelor's in elementary education, Magna Cum Laude, with a 3.9 GPA in 1982 from Southern University. Also, I was the Marshal in the College of Education.

A lot of blind people were going to college. My best friend, Teretha, went to college and graduated top of her class. She went before I did and earned a B.S. and master's in psychology. When it came to note-taking, they would tape record or ask their reader to record for

## III. SOUTHERN UNIVERSITY

them. Well, I did not want my reader taking my classes or taking my notes for me. My reader did not know what I wanted. So, I took my own notes by brailling them with my slate and stylus.

Many said I caught on exceptionally quickly in the biology lecture. If I made an A on my test, everybody wanted to see what I had for my answer. The only time I used a reader was to record my test questions and answers. There were some instructors who did not believe I could do it. So, those instructors refused to let me have a reader write for me.

One man told me, "I'll write for you myself. I'll know you didn't cheat."

He would give me an oral question, and I would answer back. He was just astonished. The whole time he thought I was relying on the reader to do everything.

I remember once taking an American History class and my teacher, Dr. Gray, would ask questions; I knew the answers to.

He asked, "When did Bienville come to Louisiana?"

I thought it was an open-ended question.

After I stated the answer, he said, "I did not ask you. It was not for you to answer."

I thought, Well, who did you ask?

One time he asked me if I felt jealous of my child because she could see and I could not. "Don't you wish you each had one good eye?"

I said, "No! Then we both would be half-blind. Why would I be jealous?"

Another time we had to go to a plantation home in St. Francisville.

He said everybody had to be independent, and we could not bring anybody with us.

Terrlyn came, so he was mad because I had brought my child, but it was a learning experience for her also.

I have had some teachers that just were narrow-minded. They were uncomfortable with me and were just being ugly.

One of my reading teachers exclaimed, "Ahh! I don't know what to do with you! I pass the test to you; you can't finish the test in time."

## III. SOUTHERN UNIVERSITY

I said, "Well, I need extra time. I need someone to read to me. Can you read to me?!"

In a snappy tone, she replied, "I don't have time to read it to you."

I exclaimed, "I don't think that is fair!"

She responded, "I don't think it's fair that I have to put up with you and your dog!"

I received a D in her class. I thought none of that made any sense. When I felt mistreated, I would go to the dean of the department because I did not think I was asking for anything special! A lot of the time, the department head would intervene.

I would not whine, but I spoke up for myself. I also had teachers that admired me.

There was one teacher who would be shaking her hand and pointing to the other students while saying, "Look at y'all, you got all these eyes and ain't got your homework! This young lady can't even see!"

I did not want to be put on a pedestal because that makes your classmates not like you.

In Ms. Parnell's method and reading class, a classmate told me that Ms. Parnell was praising me.

Ms. Parnell was asking questions about a story she had assigned for us to read. The other students did not answer many, if any, questions. But I did.

After class, the classmate said, "Girl, Ms. Parnell was giving you high praise with her hand signs. She said you was the top!"

"What you mean?" I asked.

"The whole while you were answering questions, Ms. Parnell was making hand gestures indicating you are blind and praising you while at the same time looking at the rest of us in disgrace, pity, and shame."

This was the first time I found out I was in high reverence with a teacher, simply because I was able to answer the questions. After that, whenever we had a story, the students said, "I know Mrs. Trotter knows the answer!"

Different classmates would say, "I know Mrs. Trotter is going to pass the test on Friday" or "I know she knows the characters."

However, the teacher never said anything to me or verbalized it.

## III. SOUTHERN UNIVERSITY

I had a geometry instructor who drank a lot. One day, he was explaining isosceles triangles, rectangles, and angles. I could not understand.

He implied, "If you don't understand this, you got to be blind."

I said, "I am."

He stated, "Oh, my God. I did not know!"

After class, he asked me to come to his office. He apologized profusely. None of that worried me. I never noticed prejudice due to blackness or gender. Being blind was the issue. Nobody could tolerate the blind. They did not call it visually impaired; it was just blind.

It was like, "What am I supposed to do with her?!"

"Give me an opportunity, and I'll show you what to do with me!"

A lot of people just could not understand, especially instructors.

The first person I got as a reader was paid for by vocational rehab. She was unreliable. She would never come to the library and frequently didn't show up at exam time.

A person I liked as a reader was named Betty. She was my little girl's teacher in kindergarten. Betty would pick up and drop off my daughter at the church school. I would tell Betty how hard it was to find a reader as I paid her gas money for bringing my daughter back home.

One day when she dropped my daughter off, Betty offered to read and write for me. At times, while our clothes were washing and drying in the laundromat, she would read anything I needed. If I needed something in print, she would write it for me as I dictated from my braille notes. After that, I would get someone on campus to type it. All my class work would get done.

After Betty stopped being my reader, I met another lady. Her name was Yvette. She was going to college for pre-med. One day, it was raining, and she asked me if I wanted to walk under her umbrella. It was hard to walk with a backpack, guide dog and umbrella, so I didn't have an umbrella. She and I became best friends, and then she became my reader. We stayed friends for many years.

## III. SOUTHERN UNIVERSITY

Sometimes if I was in the library and wanted to know something, I would walk up to strangers and ask them, "Could you please read this for me?"

A lot of times, the library would have the books I needed, but they would be in print. In my second and third year of college, the state library was cooperative. The library would have someone read and record my textbooks if I got them before the semester started. In my junior year, a place out of Chicago had audio books with chapters of my entire English literature textbooks, like *Othello* and Greek mythology.

Before that, I had to find people to read for me, different people all the time. Many people would be fascinated by my walking around with Kristi. I always reassured the people who helped me that Kristi would not harm them. They would always help. If it was something important, I would braille while they were reading. If I had to pay people to help me get it done, so be it. That carried on into my career.

When I first went to school, I was 27 and a freshman in college. I always tell people, "You are never too old to learn or go to college. It is never too late!"

It was a blessing that with my total blindness, vocational rehab saved me the trouble of paying tuition. Because of that I made sure to get my lesson out, be very active, and participate in all class activities.

I liked to walk in with my dog and have people wonder where we were going. I felt like I was taking part in society, like they were. No one was putting me on the side or getting this or that for me. I was getting everything for myself, and I did not have to feel indebted to anyone.

I loved the college experience. Being amongst the crowd, going to the games, especially the football games, with my daughter Terrlyn; it was very enjoyable.

There was a coach named Hightower. He would let Terrlyn and I into the games on Saturday nights. He was our swimming instructor, too. I would leave the dog at home. It was nothing for us to go to a game when they were playing at Memorial Stadium; it was down the street from my house.

Homecoming was always a big deal for Southern University. I looked forward to the homecoming activities on campus. At one time, many sororities tried to get me to join because of my grade point average. I

## III. SOUTHERN UNIVERSITY

did not join. I did not want to be told I could not go home and take care of my family. Although I was in my 20s, I was not crazy enough to think I could stay out all evening and not go home to my family. I did what I was supposed to as a mother and wife.

I rarely got lost back then. Once a dog goes so many places, they start to remember.

Kristi passed away just before my student teaching year. One day, we were on campus going to class upstairs. After class, she would not assume a guiding role. Kristi was just standing at the top of the stairs; she would not walk down. When I held her harness, she would sit down.

A schoolmate of mine said, "Hey, your dog doesn't look well. It's slobbering a lot."

We went to the veterinarian. He said, "Your dog had a stroke. She will be gone by tomorrow. She is not going to recover. I'll be glad to put her to sleep for you."

Being that he was my vet since I got Kristi, I agreed. We had been through a lot together.

One day in 1979, I let Kristi out to go relieve herself, but she did not come back. I wondered where she was, and she went missing. I was pregnant with my son and had to go to the local TV station to describe my dog. I asked if anyone had seen her and mentioned how valuable and important she was to me.

Terrlyn was nine or ten years old during this time; she was my only help to identify Kristi. We went from dumpster to dumpster searching; Kristi could have been in one, dead.

Come to find out, the person who had my dog lived right down the street from me. He said, "The dog came into my yard."

He asked for $25 as a reward for the dog. I didn't have $25 and did not pay him. I contacted the authorities.

Finally, when she did come back to me, she was very filthy. Kristi also had marks of captivity on her. She had scratches and bruises on her hips, around her tail, and around her rectum.

The police said to the guy that had Kristi, "If the dog comes up missing again, you'll be the first suspect to look for."

## III. SOUTHERN UNIVERSITY

After Kristi passed it took me less time to get ready. I didn't have to groom her. That was a plus, but I missed her companionship.

I did not want another dog. There were a lot of down sides to a dog, like having to clean her, cleaning up behind her, hair shedding, etc.

I always thought that God knew when to take Kristi because I was just getting started with student teaching. They were already against a blind person working in the public school with children. Also, a lot of kids are allergic to animals. Kristi would have been an excuse not to hire me.

I started cane travel after Kristi died. I never got as good with the cane as I did with the guide dog. A guide dog will take you around objects; you are not going to be looking for the objects. A dog is just going to go around and walk, whereas with a cane, you are always searching for the objects. If you get to a sidewalk, they will stop so you can put your foot out to step up or step down.

The main reason I did not get another dog was the area where I had to travel was not as wide. The SU campus was huge. To get from the front of the campus to the back of the campus in a timely fashion, a dog would be more advantageous. But since I was only student teaching, I would leave my house and go to the school I was assigned to. Once I got inside the school, I was inside the class. The area of my travel during the day was not as wide. Therefore, traveling with a cane wouldn't take so much time. Also, getting another dog meant we would have to get used to each other, and that could take three weeks to a month.

I went to Southern University from the spring of 1976 to the fall of 1982. I graduated with a Bachelor of Arts degree in elementary education and a minor in learning disability. Back then, they didn't give degrees in special education, so I had to spend an extra year in college. After I received my BA, I got a certification in generic education. My certification meant I could teach all disabled children, except for deaf or blind students.

A lady from the testing department read for me when my time to take the National Teacher Examination came. They would not allow me to bring a friend or anyone I knew to read for me because they thought I would cheat. A required part on the test was to know the different periods of the arts and architecture. The lady would describe the picture, and I had to tell her the era it was from. There was no

## III. SOUTHERN UNIVERSITY

Americans with Disabilities Act until 1990. Today's blind students are exempt from the pictorial portions.

What I worried about most during exam time was the required score of 800. A lot of people had made 400. All over SU's campus, people were saying the students could not pass the NTE.

I thought, geez these people can't pass. I hope I can.

Another concern was that vocational rehab told me they would only pay for me to take the test once; if I failed, too bad. At the time, it cost $100 per test.

I worried 3 times over! I scored 1100.

Along with my degrees, I got certifications to teach in Louisiana with one half semester in third grade regular education and the other half in special education. Thereafter, I received two more certifications. The first granted me to teach grade K-8 in regular education. The second was in teaching learning disabled children. Later, I got another certification in generic education which allowed me to teach emotionally, behaviorally, and mentally challenged children. Even though word got around about my 1100 test score, no teaching jobs were offered to me.

While seeking a teaching job, I worked at the nursery my son, Tyron, attended. I had him my junior year in college. At the nursery I worked with 3- and 4-year-old children. We sang songs and nursery rhymes. A woman who worked with me taught them how to form letters. We both taught them how to count. I taught them how to count by using blocks. This nursery was keeping my friend Teretha's child, too.

My job search lasted from the spring of 1983 to the fall of 1983. I never was called into a job interview until my trial session at Ryan Elementary. However, I did pursue an interview at the East Baton Rouge School Board's central office on Foster Drive in Baton Rouge. I got a taxicab there and had an interview with a lady named Ms. Sims.

After this interview, Ms. Sims said, "I got to tell you, you had one hell of an interview!"

This interview still did not get me a job. My pursuit for employment even led me across the river to Port Allen's West Baton Rouge School Board. The result was the same.

## III. SOUTHERN UNIVERSITY

I finally gained employment, on a trial basis, for East Baton Rouge Parish School System. While at Southern University, I learned if you do not speak up for yourself, no one else will. Also, a lot of times when people are hostile to you, it is not necessarily because of you personally. It is because of their own shortcomings and ignorance.

# Chapter IV

## Historical Pioneer

I got a temporary employment opportunity at Ryan Elementary from November 1983 to December 1983. A lot of sighted people could not pass the test and were not certified, yet they were making a living with temporary teaching credentials. I had a bona fide certification and could not get a job.

This school system had never had a totally blind teacher to work in East Baton Rouge Parish; therefore, they did not want to give me an opportunity until one of the school board members got on television. Mr. Millican was his name, and he talked about grouping children with low disabilities and high disabilities together.

He said, "It is better to group a lower child with a higher child academically because if you put two low children together, it would be like the blind leading the blind."

I belong to the NFB, which is short for the National Federation of the Blind. This is a national organization of blind people who speak for themselves, without others speaking for them.

The president of the local chapter of the NFB responded to the school board member's statement and said, "The comment was very derogatory, as if the blind are not capable of leading anyone."

After NFB members went to his office and explained how offensive his remarks were to blind people, Mr. Millican reappeared on television.

He said, "I'm so sorry I said demeaning statements toward the blind, and in the future, I will do what I can to help a blind person to get employed. If I can do anything in my power, I will do so."

I heard his offer. The next day, I got on the city bus, independently, and took my transcript, degrees, and NTE score to his office.

When talking to Mr. Millican, I asked, "What is holding up the parish from hiring me?" I asked why I was not considered as a future employee with a 3.9 grade point average and Class A teacher's certification.

He told me, "There's nothing holding us up, ma'am. I will do all that I can to get you the job. Let me tell you, you're going to have to learn that all of your

## IV. HISTORICAL PIONEER

little achievements are not going to get you the job. Who you know gets you the job and since you came to me, a school board member, now I can say I know you. All of your credentials will keep your job."

The school board had to discuss this matter amongst themselves. They decided to let me come to the classroom due to a teacher going on maternity leave in November. I was to work in her place between Thanksgiving and Christmas vacation. It was a whole lot of maybe this, maybe that.

My qualifications to teach were no longer the question. However, the question became if I would be a problem for the children and the parents. I had to prove I could get along in the parish.

The stipulations were until I passed their trial period of three weeks, I would have two aides instead of one. Also, I would be paid half a teacher's salary.

It was not too long before the children and parents were impressed. I brailled my material such as the student's spelling words and reading words, and I began proving myself. They remained skeptical.

I continued to have two aides with me in the classroom, unlike the sighted special education teachers, who only had one aide. One aide helped me work with the children, and the other wrote any paperwork from my dictation.

At that time, computers were not that easy to come by. What I could not get done by the end of the day, I paid out of my pocket to get private people to do for me. Sometimes, my daughter Terrlyn would write spelling words and other materials on the transparency sheets.

On my first day of the trial period, I caught two city buses to Ryan Elementary; the second bus let me off in front of the school.

The principal interviewed me. It was not at all just an interview. Mrs.Torregrossa, the principal, called it baptizing by fire. I did the whole teacher's workday, including duty. I taught classes, did recess and cafeteria duty. Everything a teacher would do in a day, I did.

Afterwards, Mrs. T, walked me to the bus stop and waited with me. Needless to say, the bus took an hour to get there. I really thought she was being a kind lady that day.

After working with her for five years, she revealed, "The first day you came, I really thought someone had

## IV. HISTORICAL PIONEER

brought you in a car. I was so tired of standing out there, but I had to know how you got here."

I stayed at Ryan Elementary throughout the fall of 1983. In the fall of 1984, the school board gave me a contract to work as a special education teacher in a self-contained classroom at Ryan Elementary. A self-contained classroom is one in which the same group of students are taught multiple subjects by one educator throughout the day.

It was a dream come true to land this job. At that point, I was allowed to work with only one aide. I also received a full salary. Like in college with my readers, I went through a series of aides, before my long-term aide, Willie B., came in November of 1984. We became fast friends, and 'til this day we are still friends.

The property was all one building until the T-buildings came. This made traveling independently on campus easy.

The children would always fuss and fight over who was going to walk me to lunch. I could walk myself, but they felt wanted and needed if I let them help me. I would put my cane away, and we held hands. A "Who's going to walk Mrs. Trotter to lunch?" list was created and placed on the wall. That list along with Music Day, field trips and a few other things, helped Ryan Elementary become a more joyful experience for us.

I loved music and we looked forward to Music Day. When the music teacher would come, we would sing some silly songs.

"Alakazamakazoo, stirring in my witches brew, I got magic," we sang. It was a Halloween song.

The music teacher's name was Mr. C. He would wobble like a duck. It was fun, really fun!

A lot of special children are not academically disabled; however, they have a lot of emotional issues.

In 1986, Mrs. Torregrossa told me, "A lot of people probably won't give you an opportunity to get tenure." Therefore, she stayed until 1990 to make sure I was treated fairly and tenured.

After a year of multiple interns, Ryan got a long-term principal named Ms. Jones.

In one of our first faculty meetings, Ms. Jones asked, "How can we stop a fight from occurring amongst students?"

## IV. HISTORICAL PIONEER

One teacher said, "As soon as the students get off the bus, send them straight to the breakfast line, so they won't have time to fight."

"That's a good idea!" Ms. Jones replied.

I suggested that the children should jump rope, play Simon Says, or play a hand-clapping game to discourage fights.

Immediately, the principal asked, "How would you know if someone was in a fight?"

"I can hear; besides, I've never seen or heard of a quiet fight," I answered.

Usually, Ms. Jones would not speak to me. Even if I was present, she would speak to my aide. I know some people are uncomfortable talking to blind people, but I soon noticed Ms. Jones had no problem criticizing me face-to-face, publicly or privately.

Once, my class got in line after the fifth graders for lunch.

Ms. Jones walked by and nearly passed us completely before she abruptly stopped. Exasperated, she stated, "There is trash on the floor here, Mrs. Trotter."

"The fifth graders did that," blurted one of my students.

"Mrs. Trotter, the next time you see paper on the floor, pick it up."

Respectfully, I said, "Yes, ma'am, the next time I SEE paper on the floor, I'll pick it up."

The whole lunchroom erupted in laughter. I always thought some of her statements and questions were silly and should have been made privately.

Our first five years working together, Ms. Jones graded my evaluations as satisfactory. However, the next year she became more challenging.

On a Wednesday, two weeks before Christmas, I was opening my classroom for the day. While unlocking the door, I heard footsteps behind me.

A voice said, "Good morning, Mrs. Trotter, how are you?"

I answered, "Good morning, Ms. Jones."

"I'm going to evaluate you today, Mrs. Trotter." She followed me inside.

## IV. HISTORICAL PIONEER

Willie B. arrived about five minutes after me, spoke to Ms. Jones, and left to meet the students. The students came in, and the school bell rang.

"Your evaluation starts now," Ms. Jones stated.

I stood in front of the class and gave instructions, and my aide wrote them on the board. If needed, I gave one-on-one assistance after that.

On this particular day, my instructions were to copy the sentence from the board and then circle the spelling words. One group was to write their words three times. The more advanced group was to make their own sentences with the spelling words. Both groups were to draw a picture using those words. One group's spelling words were "red," "toy," "snow," "tree," etc. The more advanced group's words were "Santa," "sleigh," "reindeer," etc.

Ms. Jones sat in the back row of the class, quietly observing.

We went over the spelling words like this, "The tree is tall. Which word did you circle, and how is it spelled?"

They would spell their words aloud while circling each spelling word on paper.

"What is a tree, a plant or animal? Can anyone name a type of tree? What do we do with a tree during the holidays? Can a reindeer fly? What is one special reindeer's name and why? What is a sleigh, a plant or an animal?"

They would correct me stating, "It's a thing."

"Then what do we do with a sleigh? Do we ride a sleigh in the street? Where would we ride a sleigh?"

They stated, "No, you ride it in the snow."

We continued in this format until all the spelling words were discussed. Ms. Jones whispered that she was done and quietly left the room.

I continued to follow my lesson plan for the week. I believe all subjects should be integrated as opposed to teaching each one in isolation. Thus, my method of teaching in this manner covered art, science, spelling, reading and social studies.

After lunch the following Friday, Ms. Jones saw me in the hall. As she approached, she said, "Mrs. Trotter, I would like to discuss your evaluation in a post conference."

I asked, "Now?"

## IV. HISTORICAL PIONEER

"Yes, now," she stated.

I followed her to the principal's office. Once I took a seat in her office, she closed the doors.

As Ms. Jones sat, the springs on the chair squeaked, and she shuffled through papers. Ms. Jones said, "I did not like it. I did not like it at all. First of all, your children had to look at a misspelled word on the board. Also, you failed to prepare your lesson. Next, the students were taking off their coats during evaluation. In addition, you did not stick to just your spelling words, you talked about all kinds of other stuff. I gave you all unsatisfactory on your evaluation."

"What was the misspelled word?" I asked.

"'Sleigh was the misspelled word. It was written "Sliegh;" I took 10 to 20 points off for that. You can sign here."

"Because of one word?!" I replied.

All I could think of was my students, they came first. All I ever did was prepare for my children, I worked for them and did my best every day; this was insulting.

In disbelief, I said, "No ma'am. I can't sign."

"Well, someone from the special education department will make sure that you do," she retorted.

I walked out. I didn't want to do anything I would regret, and this was the best option.

In a raspy voice and sniffling, she shouted, "Don't walk away from me! This is bigger than the both of us."

I thought to myself, if I hadn't prepared for my class, as the principal stated, then Ryan and the EBR school system had not prepared for me. This is to say, during all my years at Ryan, I brailled all my material given to me in print, even paid for it, without asking for anything.

Back in my classroom, the students were packing up to go home.

Once our students left, Willie B. asked, "How did the conference go?"

I told her about the entire encounter.

She replied, "'Sliegh'?! What?! Lord, I'm sorry."

I believed her.

I was ready to go home for the day. That evening, I called and left a voice message for my union

## IV. HISTORICAL PIONEER

representative, Mr. Vaughn. That evaluation was on my mind all weekend.

According to the Teacher's Union, she could not evaluate me on the spot. She had to give a 2-day notice beforehand. All teachers had no less than 15 minutes of preparation time prior to evaluations. Ms. Jones approached me and conversed about insignificant things during the time I could have used to prepare.

Later that week, I spoke to my union rep to plead my case. He understood and said he would share this with Ms. Jones.

He added, "Brailling all your material was a sign of preparation. With all of that in braille, who else was going to read it?! The children do not read braille. Besides, why grade you on a misspelled word written on the board by the aide?"

After our meeting, we wished each other happy holidays and went our separate ways. I was still concerned about losing my job, even though I was assured that I didn't have to worry by Mr. Vaughn. Christmas vacation was not totally enjoyable for me that year with this looming over my head.

Our first week back, after my 10:30 AM recess duty, a supervisor named Ms. Edwards was waiting for me. Ms. Edwards was from the Department of Special Education for East Baton Rouge Parish. She checked schools in her jurisdiction two to three times a year to make sure IEPs were current and accurate. IEPs are Individualized Education Plans. Most of the work she did was in office, but this particular day she wanted to visit my class and sit in on a lesson. Upon leaving, she congratulated me and talked about her exciting experience with how my students interacted with me.

About four weeks later, a lady knocked on my door, in the middle of math class.

In a friendly voice, she said, "Mrs. Trotter, I am Ms. Price, a supervisor from the central office. I was wondering if I may come in and observe."

I had never met this lady before, but I invited her in.

She stayed 30 minutes and said, "It was a wonderful lesson, and you have a remarkable rapport with your children. I enjoyed it."

I was glad everyone liked what they were observing, but I wondered what would happen to me. I thought both visits had something to do with my post conference with Ms. Jones. I continued to worry about losing my job.

Even though Ms. Jones never returned to review the evaluation, I was not at ease. I never completely stopped thinking about losing my job. It wasn't until vocational rehab, counsel for the blind, and EBR collaborated to determine how to train me and my blind coworker on doing IEPs on computers that I no longer worried about losing my job.

Later that school year, another visually impaired teacher who taught at a special school came to work at Ryan. Most of her students were wheelchair-bound with mental disabilities. She was hired in the parish with some sight, but she later lost it. East Baton Rouge and vocational rehab felt that in order to accommodate two blind teachers on staff all resources and assistance should be placed at one school; this led to her transition to Ryan Elementary. While working at Ryan, she thought the conditions I worked under were unacceptable for the both of us.

I was doing progress reports along with report cards as if my students were regular education students. Both of us did progress reports that corresponded with IEPs. She never did roll book or report cards. I was doing special ed work as well as regular ed work. Report cards go to students in regular ed, but IEPs go to students in special ed or alternative education programs.

A roll book is used as documentation for children who are enrolled in a regular education program. Everyday grades are recorded in a roll book. The grade for a report card comes from a roll book. That is for a child who is taking a regular education program. For the child in special ed or who may be addressing an alternative program, you are going to look at your IEPs. IEP objective plans are done once a year. Special ed and alternative program teachers look at this educational plan instead of a roll book. This is used to measure objective achievement. If the student has not achieved the objective, then I would put work is ongoing.

At Ryan, I did both because Ms. Jones said parents want to see students with report cards. If we gave a child an A we, the special ed teachers, would have to specify the grade level of the "A". For example, first grade level, second grade level or third grade level "A" and so forth.

## IV. HISTORICAL PIONEER

Before the end of April, I had another visitor from vocational rehab. This man said he was called in by our parish school system. He happened to come by while my students were at P.E. He informed me that vocational rehab had considered collaborating with the parish to train the blind teachers in using computers.

East Baton Rouge Parish School System no longer wanted a handwritten IEP. A program was in development to teach sighted teachers how to move from handwritten to online IEPs. There was no one in the parish who knew how to teach the blind teachers. Also, funding was in question. Over the summer, they discussed ways to accommodate my blind co-worker and me. However, it could not be done until after June 30th; that was the beginning of the new budget.

The entire 1996 school year was more disheartening. I returned to Ryan, but Willie B. and Ms. Jones were assigned to another school. I had a new aide named Mrs. Robinson. We got along well, better than Willie B. in some aspects.

Willie B. was the type of person who worked like a mama overseeing. She had been teaching for 15 to 20 years when I started. She dealt with things in an old-time, country kind of way. Sometimes when I gave instructions in a proper grammatical way, my students would not understand what I meant. Willie B. could break it down simply. She inserted her ideas often, and they usually worked. Willie B. was as helpful as she could be and meant well.

On the other hand, Mrs. Robinson was very professional. We worked like a hand and glove team. I was the teacher, and she would wait for my lead. If I asked Mrs. Robinson for her opinion; she would give it to me.

Mrs. Robinson and I had some challenging students.

One of my students told me that if I did not let him go to recess he would bring his .22 for me when he returned to school. In my attempts to show him somebody cared, I did not report him. I was never afraid of students. My biggest fear was correcting a student with corporal punishment and getting in trouble for it. All my hard work would go down the drain. This student had been in enough trouble.

In another incident that year, a female student came in my class. She had a bag in her hand and said, "Good morning, Mrs. Trotter. I have some cookies for you. I baked them."

## IV. HISTORICAL PIONEER

Surprised, I said, "You did? Thank you."

While she was handing me the bag, Mrs. Robinson intercepted the cookies and said, "What is this? These cookies aren't real. You did not bake these! These are made out of mud! Mrs. Trotter, you really should report her. She should not be giving you dirt cookies!"

I asked if they were dirt cookies, and the student started to cry. "I just wanted to play a trick on Mrs. Trotter and see if she would know if they were real or not."

I did not report her even though I was disheartened.

In May of 1997, vocational rehab decided that my co-worker and I would go to a center for the blind in Lafayette, LA. We started mid-June of 1997 and stayed for three weeks. It was a dormitory setting. Our classes were from 8 AM to 3 PM. We learned Windows '95, keyboarding and a program named JAWS.

JAWS is a computer screen reader program for Microsoft Windows that was released in January 1995. It allows blind and visually impaired users to read the screen either with a text-to-speech output or by a refreshable braille display.

On weekends, I caught a ride with my co-worker and her husband back to Baton Rouge. I hated leaving my little 9 year old, Kryston. She cried for me whenever I went back to Lafayette.

I was glad to get back home from my training and excited about the new school year. We learned so much and were ready to show it! Once we got back to school, it was painfully obvious the program we learned in Lafayette was not compatible with the IEP program in this parish. The school system said they were going to get us computers for school use, but we never saw them. My blind co-worker and I could not do the job with their computers without the blind-friendly software.

In June 1998, my co-worker and I retired on disability. My employment at Ryan Elementary spanned from fall 1984 to summer 1998.

It was challenging. Some of my challenges were always getting materials for my students then brailling, so I could read along with them. However, I enjoyed my time at Ryan. I did everything that a special education teacher in this parish could do. There was

## IV. HISTORICAL PIONEER

nothing like it. I loved my students, and my students loved me. On duty, I would jump rope and play slide with them. Sighted and blind could enjoy the auditorium, gym, and classrooms. Working at Ryan was enjoyable.

We had motivational speakers come and talk to the children. A guy named Cleo Fields, a former congressman, once spoke to us. He told the students the same thing I did in class every day.

"In life, there is no special ed, you gon' get your electric bills. Whether you can see, walk, talk, or hear. Moreover, your house note will need to be paid. If you gon' function in a society, you got to measure up. Sometimes you got to work double time, triple time to get it done. Nobody gives you anything in this world. You have to earn it."

My class went on many field trips and walked in a Mardi Gras parade. On one of the field trips, we used the city bus system with my aide and went to the state capital. After that, we had lunch and went back to school on the city bus. On another field trip for social studies, we went on a boat called, *Samuel Clemens*. It was a little excursion boat on the Mississippi River, traveling from the base of downtown Baton Rouge to

Louisiana State University and back. We never took a plane ride, but we did go to the airport to see planes. At that time, we could meet pilots and go inside the plane.

Ryan was a welcome and much needed escape from my home life at times. While employed at Ryan, I divorced my first husband of 17 years.

I had a beautiful little girl. Her father was a postman and a World War II veteran. He began to come around after my divorce. I did not pursue him before my annulment. Postman Brown assisted my oldest child in learning how to drive. I really loved him. However, he was in a 30-year marriage that neither of us wanted him to leave.

Consequently, I went on to find my second husband. He was an alcoholic that didn't keep any steady work. I cared for him and thought I could help him. There were nights when he would be furious with my son Tyron and I.

Often, the night before school, we would wash school clothes. My husband would unplug the washer and dryer while yelling, "I'm trying to get some f'in sleep!"

## IV. HISTORICAL PIONEER

Once, he pistol-whipped me. I called the police, and they took him away. That same day, my brother Bill called to inform me that Mama Emma died. All of that happened prior to my retirement from Ryan. None of that kept me from performing my duties as a teacher.

Being a teacher was indeed a dream come true. It was a privilege to teach sighted students and give valuable tools for them to use in their future.

Thank you all! Special thanks to my children, grandchildren and my great-grandchildren. I love you.

www.ingramcontent.com/pod-product-compliance
Lightning Source LLC
Chambersburg PA
CBHW031407040426
42444CB00005B/449